# Just for
# Kids

## 31 Daily Devotions

# Sharing

*The quoted ideas expressed in this book (but not scripture verses) are not, in all cases, exact quotations, as some have been edited for clarity and brevity. In all cases, the author has attempted to maintain the speaker's original intent. In some cases, quoted material for this book was obtained from secondary sources, primarily print media. While every effort was made to ensure the accuracy of these sources, the accuracy cannot be guaranteed. For additions, deletions, corrections or clarifications in future editions of this text, please write FAMILY CHRISTIAN PRESS.*

Scripture quotations are taken from:

The Holy Bible, King James Version

The Holy Bible, New International Version (NIV) Copyright © 1973, 1978, 1984, by International Bible Society. Used by permission of Zondervan Publishing House. All rights reserved.

The Holy Bible, New King James Version (NKJV) Copyright © 1982 by Thomas Nelson, Inc. Used by permission.

The New American Standard Bible®, (NASB) Copyright © 1960, 1962, 1963, 1968, 1971, 1972, 1973, 1975, 1977, 1995 by The Lockman Foundation. Used by permission.

Holy Bible, New Living Translation, (NLT)copyright © 1996. Used by permission of Tyndale House Publishers, Inc., Wheaton, Illinois 60189. All rights reserved.

The Message (MSG)- This edition issued by contractual arrangement with NavPress, a division of The Navigators, U.S.A. Originally published by NavPress in English as THE MESSAGE: The Bible in Contemporary Language copyright 2002-2003 by Eugene Peterson. All rights reserved.

New Century Version®. (NCV) Copyright © 1987, 1988, 1991 by Word Publishing, a division of Thomas Nelson, Inc. All rights reserved. Used by permission.

The Holman Christian Standard Bible™ (HCSB) Copyright © 1999, 2000, 2001 by Holman Bible Publishers. Used by permission.

International Children's Bible®, New Century Version®. (ICB) Copyright © 1986, 1988, 1999 by Tommy Nelson™, a division of Thomas Nelson, Inc. All rights reserved. Used by permission.

Cover Design by Kim Russell / Wahoo Designs
Page Layout by Bart Dawson

ISBN 1-58334-304-0

*Printed in the United States of America*

# Just for Kids

# Kids

# Sharing

# Table of Contents

# A Message for Parents

If your child's bookshelf is already spilling over with a happy assortment of good books for kids, congratulations—that means you're a thoughtful parent who understands the importance of reading to your child.

This little book is an important addition to your child's library. It is intended to be read by Christian parents to their young children. The text contains 31 brief chapters, one for each day of the month. Each chapter consists of a Bible verse, a brief story or lesson, kid-friendly quotations from notable Christian thinkers, a tip, and a prayer. Every chapter examines a different aspect of an important Biblical theme: sharing.

For the next 31 days, take the time to read one chapter each night to your child, and then spend a few moments talking about the chapter's meaning. By the end of the month, you will have had 31 different opportunities to share God's wisdom with your son or daughter, and that's good . . . very good.

If you have been touched by God's love and His grace, then you know the joy that He has brought into your own life. Now it's your turn to share His message with the boy or girl whom He has entrusted to your care. Happy reading! And may God richly bless you and your family now and forever.

# Sharing Is God's Way

If you have two coats, give one to
the poor. If you have food,
share it with those who are hungry.

Luke 3:11 NLT

You've heard it plenty of times from your parents and teachers: share your things. But it's important to realize that sharing isn't just something that grown-ups want you to do. It's also something that God wants you to do.

The word "possessions" is another way of describing the stuff that belongs to you: your clothes, your toys, your books, and things like that are "your possessions."

Jesus says that you should learn how to share your possessions without feeling bad about it. Sometimes, of course, it's very hard to share and very easy to be stingy. But God wants you to share—and to keep sharing! Since that's what God wants, it's what you should want, too.

Nothing is really ours until we share it.

C. S. Lewis

How generous you are does not depend
on how much you give,
but how much you have left.

Anonymous

# Tip of the Day

What does the Bible say about sharing our
possessions? The Bible answers this question
very clearly: when other people need our help,
we should gladly share the things we have.

# Prayer of the Day

Dear Lord, I know there is
no happiness in keeping Your blessings
for myself. Today, I will share
my blessings with my family,
with my friends, and people
who need my help.
Amen

# The Golden Rule

Do to others what you want them
to do to you.
Matthew 7:12 NCV

D o you want other people to share with you? Of course you do. And that's why you should share with them. The words of Matthew 7:12 remind us that, as believers in Christ, we should treat others as we wish to be treated. And that means that we should share our things with others.

The Golden Rule is your tool for deciding how you will treat other people. When you use the Golden Rule as your guide for living, your words and your actions will be pleasing to other people and to God.

We are never more like God than
when we give.

Charles Swindoll

The happiest and most joyful people are
those who give money and serve.

Dave Ramsey

# Tip of the Day

How would you feel if you were that person?
When you're trying to decide how to treat
another person, ask yourself this question:
"How would I feel if somebody treated me
that way?" Then, treat the other person the
way that you would want to be treated.

# Prayer of the Day

Dear Lord, help me always to do
my very best to treat others as
I wish to be treated. The Golden Rule
is Your rule, Father;
let me also make it mine.
Amen

# What the Bible Says

Your word is a lamp to my feet
and a light for my path.
Psalm 119:105 NIV

What book contains everything that God has to say about sharing? The Bible, of course. If you read the Bible every day, you'll soon be convinced that sharing is very important to God. And, since sharing is important to God, it should be important to you, too.

The Bible is the most important book you'll ever own. It's God's Holy Word. Read it every day, and follow its instructions. If you do, you'll be safe now and forever.

Some read the Bible to learn,
and some read the Bible to hear from heaven.

Andrew Murray

Don't worry about what you do not
understand of the Bible. Worry about what
you do understand and do not live by.

Corrie ten Boom

## Tip of the Day

Read the Bible? Every Day! Try to read your
Bible with your parents every day. If they
forget, remind them!

# Prayer of the Day

Dear Lord, the Bible is Your gift
to me. I will use it, I will trust it,
and I will obey it, today
and every day that I live.
Amen

# Sharing with Friends

A friend loves you all the time,
and a brother helps in time of trouble.

Proverbs 17:17 NCV

How can you be a good friend? One way is by sharing. And here are some of the things you can share: smiles, kind words, pats on the back, your toys, school supplies, books, and, of course, your prayers.

Would you like to make your friends happy? And would you like to make yourself happy at the same time? Here's how: treat your friends like you want to be treated. That means obeying the Golden Rule, which, of course, means sharing. In fact, the more you share, the better friend you'll be.

A friend is the hope of the heart.

Ralph Waldo Emerson

Friends are angels who lift our feet
when our own wings have trouble
remembering how to fly.

Anonymous

## Tip of the Day

Want to make friends? Pay attention! The
more interested you are in them, the more
interested they will become in you!

# Prayer of the Day

Dear Lord, thank You for my friends.
Let me be a good friend to
other people, and let me show them
what it means to be a good Christian.
Amen

# Sharing with Family

Let them first learn to do their duty to
their own family and to repay their parents
or grandparents. That pleases God.

1 Timothy 5:4 NCV

A good place to start sharing is at home—but it isn't always an easy place to start. Sometimes, especially when we're tired or mad, we don't treat our family members as nicely as we should. And that's too bad!

Do you have brothers and sisters? Or cousins? If so, you're lucky.

Sharing your things—without whining or complaining—is a wonderful way to show your family that you love them. So the next time a brother or sister or cousin asks to borrow something, say "yes" without getting mad. It's a great way to say, "I love you."

You leave home to seek your fortune
and when you get it you go home
and share it with your family.

Anita Baker

You don't choose your family.
They are God's gift to you,
as you are to them.

Desmond Tutu

# Tip of the Day

Since you love your family . . . let them know
it by the things you say and the things you
do. And, never take your family members
for granted; they deserve your very best
treatment!

## Prayer of the Day

Dear Lord, You have given me a family
that cares for me and loves me.
Thank You. I will let my family
know that I love them by the things
that I say and do. You know that
I love my family, Lord.
Now it's my turn to show them!
Amen

# When Sharing Is Hard

Remember the words of Jesus. He said,
"It is more blessed to give than to receive."
Acts 20:35 ICB

Jesus said, "It is more blessed to give than to receive." That means that we should be generous with other people—but sometimes we don't feel much like sharing. Instead of sharing the things that we have, we want to keep them all to ourselves. That's when we must remember that God doesn't want selfishness to rule our hearts; He wants us to be generous.

Are you lucky enough to have nice things? If so, God's instructions are clear: you must share your blessings with others. And that's exactly the way it should be. After all, think how generous God has been with you.

From what we get, we can make a living;
what we give, however, makes a life.

Arthur Ashe

The happiest people are those who
do the most for others.

Booker T. Washington

# Tip of the Day

Kindness every day: Kindness should be part
of our lives every day, not just on the days
when we feel good. Don't try to be kind some
of the time, and don't try to be kind to some
of the people you know. Instead, try to be
kind all of the time, and try to be kind to all
of the people you know.

# Prayer of the Day

Dear Lord, it's easy to share with some people and difficult to share with others. Let me be kind to all people so that I might follow in the footsteps of Your Son.

Amen

# God Sees the Heart

We justify our actions by appearances;
God examines our motives.
Proverbs 21:2 MSG

Other people see you from the outside. God sees you from the inside—God sees your heart.

Kindness comes from the heart. So does sharing. So if you want to show your family and your friends that your heart is filled with kindness and love, one way to do it is by sharing. But don't worry about trying to show God what kind of person you are. He already knows your heart, and He loves you more than you can imagine.

He is always thinking about us.
We are before his eyes. The Lord's eye never
sleeps, but is always watching out for
our welfare. We are continually on his heart.

C. H. Spurgeon


God does not work in all hearts alike,
but according to the preparation
and sensitivity the Creator finds in each.

Meister Eckhart

# Tip of the Day

Talk about your feelings: If something is
bothering you, tell your parents. Don't be
afraid to talk about your feelings. Your mom
and dad love you, and they can help you. So
whatever "it" is, talk about it . . . with your
parents!

# Prayer of the Day

Dear Lord, thank You for loving me.
I will return Your love by sharing it . . .
today and every day.
Amen

# The Best Time to Share

Always try to do what is good for each other and for all people.

1 Thessalonians 5:15 ICB

When is the best time to share? Whenever you can—and that means right now, if possible. When you start thinking about the things you can share, you probably think mostly about things that belong to you (like toys or clothes), but there are many more things you can share (like love, kindness, encouragement, and prayers). That means you have the opportunity to share something with somebody almost any time you want. And that's exactly what God wants you to do—so start sharing now and don't ever stop.

Do noble things,
do not dream them all day long.

Charles Kingsley

God has lots of folks who intend to go
to work for him "some day."
What He needs is more people who
are willing to work for Him this day.

Marie T. Freeman

## Tip of the Day

How about sharing a hug right now? The
person who's reading you this book deserves
one!

# Prayer of the Day

Dear Lord, there are so many things
that I can share. Help me never to
forget the importance of sharing
my possessions, my prayers,
and my love with family members
and friends.
Amen

# How They Know You're a Christian

My dear friends, don't believe everything
you hear. Carefully weigh and examine
what people tell you. Not everyone who
talks about God comes from God.

1 John 4:1 MSG

How do people know that you're a Christian? Well, you can tell them, of course. And make no mistake about it: talking about your faith in God is a very good thing to do. But telling people about Jesus isn't enough. You should also show people how a Christian (like you) should behave.

God wants you to be loving and giving. That way, when another person sees how you behave, that person will know what it means to be a good Christian . . . a good Christian like you!

A person ought to live so that everybody knows he is a Christian.

D. L. Moody

For what we dare to give to one another in love enriches us at the time, stays behind to comfort and help at our parting, yet still goes on to heaven—a seed to flower in eternity, bringing perennial joy.

Susan Lenzkes

# Tip of the Day

Christians are . . . kind and respectful: As a Christian, you must make sure that you show proper respect for everyone, even if that person happens to be different from you. It's easy to make fun of people who seem different . . . but it's wrong.

# Prayer of the Day

Dear Lord, help me to make
Your world a better place. I can't fix
all the world's troubles, but I can help
make things better with kind words,
good deeds, and sincere prayers.
Let my actions and my prayers
be pleasing to You, Lord,
now and forever.
Amen

# The Stuff You Don't Need

Those who trust in riches will be ruined.
But a good person will be as healthy
as a green leaf.

Proverbs 11:28 ICB

D o you have more toys than you can play with? Do you have clothes that you no longer like to wear? If so, it's time to start thinking about who could use them.

Talk to your parents about ways to share the things you aren't using. Remember this: somebody out there would gladly use these things; in fact, somebody out there needs these things. And it's up to you and your parents to find that somebody—and share.

There is absolutely no evidence that
complexity and materialism lead to happiness.
On the contrary, there is plenty of evidence
that simplicity and spirituality lead to joy,
a blessedness that is better than happiness.

Dennis Swanberg

Outside appearances, things like the clothes
you wear or the car you drive, are important
to other people but totally unimportant
to God. Trust God.

Marie T. Freeman

## Tip of the Day

Finding loving homes for clothes and toys:
your parents can help you find younger
children who need the clothes and toys that
you've outgrown.

## Prayer of the Day

Dear Lord, help me make Your world a better place. I can't fix all the world's troubles, but I can make things better here at home. Help me remember the importance of sharing the things that I have and the importance of sharing the love that I feel in my heart.

Amen

# Learning to Share

I tell you the truth, whatever you did
for one of the least of these brothers
of mine, you did for me.

Matthew 25:40 NIV

If you're having a little trouble learning how to share your stuff, you're not alone! Most people have problems letting go of things, so don't be discouraged. Just remember that learning to share requires practice and lots of it. The more you share—and the more you learn how good it feels to share—the sooner you'll be able to please God with the generosity and love that flows from your heart.

Begin to know Christ now, and finish never.

Oswald Chambers

And every gift, though it be small,
is in reality great if given with affection.

Pindar

## Tip of the Day

Practice, Practice, Practice: Want to get good at sharing? Start by sharing little things, and work your way up from there.

## Prayer of the Day

Dear Lord, help me to learn
the importance of sharing. The Bible
teaches me to share, and so do
my parents. Now, it's up to me to
learn how to share the things that
I have—and it's up to me to share
kind words and good deeds with
my family and friends.
Amen

# It Makes You a Better Person

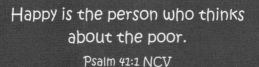

Happy is the person who thinks
about the poor.
Psalm 41:1 NCV

It's a fact: sharing makes you a better person. Why? Because when you share, you're doing several things: first, you're obeying God; and, you're making your corner of the world a better place; and you're learning exactly what it feels like to be a generous, loving person.

When you share, you have the fun of knowing that your good deeds are making other people happy. When you share, you're learning how to become a better person. When you share, you're making things better for other people and for yourself. So do the right thing: share!

A candle loses nothing of its light
by lighting another candle.

James Keller

Happiness is obedience to God.

C. H. Spurgeon

## Tip of the Day

Would you like to be a little happier? The
Bible says that if you become a more generous
person, you'll become a happier person, too.

## Prayer of the Day

Dear Lord, I can't really enjoy
my blessings until I share them.
Let me learn to be a generous person,
and let me say "thanks" to You by
sharing some of the gifts that
You have already given me.
Amen

# Kindness Counts

A kind person is doing himself a favor.
But a cruel person brings
trouble upon himself.

Proverbs 11:17 ICB

King Solomon was the man who wrote most of the Book of Proverbs; in it, he gave us lots of helpful advice. Solomon warned that unkind behavior leads only to trouble, but kindness is its own reward.

The next time you're tempted to say or do something unkind, remember Solomon. He was one of the wisest men who ever lived, and he knew that it's always better to be kind. And now, you know it, too.

If we have the true love of God in our hearts,
we will show it in our lives.

D. L. Moody

Scatter seeds of kindness.

George Ade

# Tip of the Day

You can't just talk about it: In order to
be a kind person, you must do kind things.
Thinking about them isn't enough. So get
busy! The day to start being a more generous
person is today!

# Prayer of the Day

Dear Lord, help me to be a kind and generous person. The Bible tells me to share my things. I won't wait to share them; I will share them now.
Amen

# Learning from Jesus

Mary was sitting at Jesus' feet
and listening to him teach.

Luke 10:39 ICB

Who was the greatest teacher in the history of the world? Jesus was . . and He still is! Jesus teaches us how to live, how to behave, and how to worship. Now, it's up to each of us, as Christians, to learn the important lessons that Jesus can teach.

Some day soon, you will have learned everything that Jesus has to teach you, right? WRONG!!!! Jesus will keep teaching you important lessons throughout your life. And that's good, because all of us, kids and grown-ups alike, have lots to learn . . . especially from the Master . . . and the Master, of course, is Jesus.

There is not a single thing that Jesus cannot change, control, and conquer because He is the living Lord.

Franklin Graham

Nobody ever outgrows the Bible; the book widens and deepens with our years.

C. H. Spurgeon

# Tip of the Day

Learning about Jesus: Start learning about Jesus, and keep learning about Him as long as you live. His story never grows old, and His teachings never fail.

## Prayer of the Day

Dear Lord, You are my Teacher.
Help me to learn from You. And then,
let me show others what it means to
be a kind, generous, loving Christian.
Amen

# Solomon Says

Here is my final advice:
Honor God and obey his commands.

Ecclesiastes 12:13 ICB

Solomon wasn't just a king. He was also a very wise man and a very good writer. He even wrote several books in the Bible! So when He finally put down His pen, what was this wise man's final advice? It's simple: Solomon said, "Honor God and obey His commandments."

The next time you have an important choice to make, ask yourself this: "Am I honoring God and obeying Him? And am I doing what God wants me to do?" If you can answer those questions with a great big "YES," then go ahead. But if you're uncertain if the choice you are about to make is the right one, slow down. Why? Because that's what Solomon says . . . and that's what God says, too!

The more wisdom enters our hearts,
the more we will be able to trust our hearts
in difficult situations.

John Eldredge

God's mark is on everything that obeys Him.

Martin Luther

# Tip of the Day

Simon says? Solomon says! Have you ever played the game Simon Says? When you play it, you're not supposed to move until the leader calls out, "Simon Says!" Wise King Solomon had many rules for living. You should get to know those rules—especially the ones that are golden.

## Prayer of the Day

Dear Lord, when I play by Your rules,
You give me wonderful rewards.
I will read the Bible, Lord,
so I can learn Your rules—and I will
obey Your rules, today and always.
Amen

# It's a Habit

Do not be misled:
"Bad company corrupts good character."
1 Corinthians 15:33 NIV

Our lives are made up of lots and lots of habits. These habits help determine the kind of people we become. If we choose habits that are good, we are happier and healthier. If we choose habits that are bad, then it's too bad for us!

Sharing, like so many other things, is a habit. And it's a habit that is right for you.

Do you want to grow up to become the kind of person that God intends for you to be? Then get into the habit of sharing the gifts that your Heavenly Father has given you. You'll be glad you did . . . and so will God!

Prayer is a habit. Worship is a habit.
Kindness is a habit. And if you want
to please God, you'd better make sure
that these habits are your habits.

Marie T. Freeman


Make good habits and they will make you.

Parks Cousins


## Tip of the Day

Choose your habits carefully: habits are
easier to make than they are to break, so be
careful!

# Prayer of the Day

Dear Lord, help me form good habits.
And let me make a habit of sharing
the things that I own and the love
that I feel in my heart.
Amen

# Sharing with Your Church

For we are God's fellow workers;
you are God's field, you are God's building.
1 Corinthians 3:9 NKJV

When the offering plate passes by, are you old enough to drop anything in it? If you are, congratulations! But if you're not quite old enough to give money to the church, don't worry—there are still lots of things you can share!

Even when you don't have money to share, you still have much to give to your church. What are some things you can share? Well, you can share your smile, your happiness, your laughter, your energy, your cooperation, your prayers, your obedience, your example, and your love.

So don't worry about giving to the church: even if you don't have lots of money, there are still plenty of ways you can give. And the best time to start giving is NOW!

Joyful living means joyful giving.

E. Stanley Jones

The church is where it's at.
The first place of Christian service for
any Christian is in a local church.

Jerry Clower

# Tip of the Day

Got Money? Share It! Have you ever earned
money for doing things around the house? Or
have you ever received money as a gift? If so,
ask your parents to help you decide on the
best way to share some of it.

## Prayer of the Day

Dear Lord, thank You for my church.
When I am at church, I will be
generous, kind, well-behaved,
and respectful. And when I am not
at church, I will act the same way.
Amen

# Too Young to Share?

Get the word out. Teach all these things.
And don't let anyone put you down
because you're young. Teach believers
with your life: by word, by demeanor,
by love, by faith, by integrity.

1 Timothy 4:11-12 MSG

How old should you be before you should start learning how to share your stuff? If you're old enough to understand these words (and you are!), then you're plenty old enough to learn how to become a person who cooperates and shares.

Have you noticed that small babies aren't very good at sharing? No wonder! They're too young to know better—but you're not. So do what you know is right: share!

We have a powerful potential in our young people, and we must have the courage to change old ideas and practices so that we may direct their power toward good ends.

Mary McLeod Bethune

The maturity of a Christian cannot be reached in a moment. All of us are growing up in Christ.

Hannah Whitall Smith

## Tip of the Day

With more birthdays comes better behavior: as you grow up, you'll keep learning better ways to behave yourself. The more candles on your birthday cake, the better you'll be expected to behave—and the easier it will become to behave yourself.

## Prayer of the Day

Dear Lord, while I am growing up,
I still have so many things to learn.
Let me remember that
the most important lessons are
the ones that I learn every day
from my parents and from You.
Amen

# When Others Don't Share

I tell you, love your enemies. Pray for those who hurt you. If you do this, you will be true sons of your Father in heaven.

Matthew 6:44-45 ICB

Face it: sometimes people aren't nice. And when other people don't share, you may be tempted to strike out in anger. Don't do it! Instead, remember that God corrects other people's behaviors in His own way, and He probably doesn't need your help. And remember that God has commanded you to forgive other people, just as you seek forgiveness from others when you misbehave. So, when other people aren't nice, forgive them as quickly as you can. And leave the rest up to God.

Nothing is really ours until we share it.

C. S. Lewis

Let this be thy whole endeavor,
this thy prayer, this thy desire—that
thou mayest be stripped of all selfishness,
and with entire simplicity follow Jesus only.

Thomas à Kempis

## Tip of the Day

Count to ten . . . but don't stop there! If
you're angry with someone, don't say the first
thing that comes to your mind. Instead, catch
your breath and start counting until you are
once again in control of your temper. If you
get to a million and you're still counting, go to
bed! You'll feel better in the morning.

## Prayer of the Day

Lord, when I become angry, help me
to remember that You offer me peace.
Let me turn to You for wisdom,
for patience, and for the peace
that only You can give.
Amen

# Sharing Cheerfully

God loves a cheerful giver.
2 Corinthians 9:7 NIV

How many times have you heard someone say, "Don't touch that; it's mine!" If you're like most of us, you've heard those words many times and you may have even said them yourself.

The Bible tells us that it's better for us to share things than it is to keep them all to ourselves. And the Bible also tells us that when we share, it's best to do so cheerfully. So today and every day, let's share. It's the best way because it's God's way.

Selfishness is as far from Christianity as darkness is from light.

C. H. Spurgeon

Giving unselfishly to our own families tests the true heart of a servant of God.

Mother Teresa

## Tip of the Day

When am I old enough to start giving? If you're old enough to understand these words, you're old enough to start giving to your church and to those who are less fortunate than you. If you're not sure about the best way to do it, ask your parents!

# Prayer of the Day

Dear Lord, thank You for loving me.
I will return Your love by sharing it . . .
today and every day.
Amen

# It's Tempting to Be Selfish

When you do things, do not let selfishness or pride be your guide. Be humble and give more honor to others than to yourselves.

Philippians 2:3 ICB

It's tempting to be selfish, but it's wrong. It's tempting to want to keep everything for yourself, but it's better to share. It's tempting to say, "No, that's MINE!" but it's better to say, "I'll share it with you."

Are you sometimes tempted to be a little stingy? Are you sometimes tempted to say, "No, I don't' want to share that!"—and then do you feel a little sorry that you said it? If that describes you, don't worry: everybody is tempted to be a little bit selfish. Your job is to remember this: even when it's tempting to be selfish, you should try very hard not to be. Because when you're generous, not selfish, you'll make your parents proud and you'll make your Father in Heaven proud, too.

The great danger for family life, in the midst
of any society whose idols are pleasure,
comfort and independence,
lies in the fact that people close their
hearts and become selfish.

Pope John Paul II

## Tip of the Day

Tempted to get into an argument? Walk away.
The best fights are those that never happen.

# Prayer of the Day

Dear Lord, Your Son Jesus
was never selfish. Let me follow
in His footsteps by sharing with
those who need my help.
Amen

# Let Your Light Shine

You are the light of the world.
Matthew 5:14 NIV

The Bible says that you are "the light that gives light to the world." The Bible also says that you should live in a way that lets other people understand what it means to be a good person. And of course, learning to share is an important part of being a good person.

What kind of "light" have you been giving off? Hopefully, you have been a good example for everybody to see. Why? Because the world needs all the light it can get, and that includes your light, too!

It is a great deal better to live
a holy life than to talk about it.
Lighthouses do not ring bells, they just shine.

D. L Moody

Light is stronger than darkness—
darkness cannot "comprehend"
or "overcome" it.

Anne Graham Lotz

## Tip of the Day

Let your light shine by being respectful:
Everybody is important to God. And you
should treat every person with courtesy,
dignity and respect.

## Prayer of the Day

Dear Lord, let my light shine brightly for You. Let me be a good example for all to see, and let me share love and kindness with my family and friends, today and every day.

Amen

# The Good Samaritan

Help each other with your troubles.
When you do this,
you truly obey the law of Christ.

Galatians 6:2 ICB

Sometimes we would like to help make the world a happier place, but we're not sure how to do it. Jesus told the story of the "Good Samaritan," a man who helped a fellow traveler when no one else would. We, too, should be good Samaritans when we find people who need our help.

So what can you do to make God's world a better place? You can start by making your own corner of the world a little nicer place to live (by sharing kind words and good deeds). And then, you can take your concerns to God in prayer. Whether you've offered a helping hand or a heartfelt prayer, you've done a lot.

When somebody needs a helping hand,
he doesn't need it tomorrow or the next day.
He needs it now, and that's exactly when you
should offer to help. Good deeds, if they are
really good, happen sooner rather than later.

Marie T. Freeman

You cannot cure your sorrow by
nursing it; but you can cure it by
nursing another's sorrow.

George Matheson

## Tip of the Day

Does a friend or family member need your
help? Then be a Good Samaritan by sharing
a helping hand, a friendly word, or a happy
smile.

# Prayer of the Day

Dear Lord, when my family or friends need me, let me behave myself like the Good Samaritan. Let me be helpful, generous, and kind . . . today, tomorrow, and every day of my life.

Amen

# You'll Feel Better about Yourself

So think clearly and exercise self-control.
Look forward to the special blessings
that will come to you at the return
of Jesus Christ.

1 Peter 1:13 NLT

The more you share, the quicker you'll discover this fact: Good things happen to people (like you) who are kind enough to share the blessings that God has given them.

Sharing makes you feel better about yourself. Whether you're at home or at school, remember that the best rewards go to the kids who are kind and generous—not to the people who are unkind or stingy. So do what's right: share. You'll feel lots better about yourself when you do.

Stop blaming yourself and feeling guilty, unworthy, and unloved. Instead begin to say, "If God is for me, who can be against me? God loves me, and I love myself. Praise the Lord, I am free in Jesus' name, amen!"

Joyce Meyer

It is one of the most beautiful compensations of life that no one can sincerely try to help another without helping herself.

Barbara Johnson

## Tip of the Day

Feeling better about yourself by helping other people: When talking to other people, ask yourself this question: "How helpful can I be?" When you help others, you'll be proud of yourself, and God will be, too!

# Prayer of the Day

Dear Lord, help me to slow down and to think about my behavior. And then, help me to do the right thing, so that I can feel better about myself . . . and You can, too. Amen

# You're an Example

In every way be an example of
doing good deeds.

Titus 2:7 NCV

What kind of example are you? Are you the kind of person who shows other people what it means to share? Hopefully you are that kind of person!!!

Whether you realize it or not, you're an example to your friends and family members. So today, be a good example for others to follow. Because God needs people (like you) who are willing to behave themselves as God intends. And that's exactly the kind of example you should always try to be.

Do all the good you can. In all the ways you can. In all the places you can. At all the times you can. To all the people you can. As long as you can.

John Wesley

Example is a lesson that all can read.

Gilbert West

## Tip of the Day

Your friends are watching: so be the kind of example that God wants you to be—be a good example.

# Prayer of the Day

Lord, make me a good example to
my family and friends. Let the things
that I say and do show everybody what
it means to be a good person
and a good Christian.
Amen

# God Knows

I, the Lord, examine the mind, I test the heart to give to each according to his way, according to what his actions deserve.

Jeremiah 17:10 HCSB

Even when nobody else is watching, God is. Nothing that we say or do escapes the watchful eye of our Father in heaven.

God understands that we are not perfect, but even though He knows that we make mistakes, He still wants us to live according to His rules, not our own.

The next time that you're tempted to say something that you shouldn't say or to do something that you shouldn't do, remember that you can't keep secrets from God. So don't even try!

When we are in the presence of God,
removed from distractions, we are able
to hear him more clearly, and a secure
environment has been established for
the young and broken places
in our hearts to surface.

John Eldredge

God is every moment totally aware of
each one of us. Totally aware in intense
concentration and love. No one passes
through any area of life, happy or tragic,
without the attention of God with Him.

Eugenia Price

# Tip of the Day

Big, bigger, and very big plans. God has very
big plans in store for you, so trust Him, and
do your best to obey His rules.

## Prayer of the Day

Dear Lord, You know my heart.
And, You have given me a conscience
that tells me what is right and what is
wrong. I will listen to that quiet voice
so I can do the right thing
today and every day.
Amen

# Helping Others Is Fun

Happy is the person who . . .
loves what the Lord commands.

Psalm 112:1 ICB

Helping other people can be fun! When you help others, you feel better about yourself. And, you know that God approves of what you're doing.

When you learn how to cooperate with your family and friends, you'll soon discover that it's more fun when everybody works together. And one way that you can all work together is by sharing.

So do yourself a favor: learn better ways to share and to cooperate. It's the right thing to do, and besides: it's more fun.

Make it a rule, and pray to God to help you to keep it, never, if possible, to lie down at night without being able to say: "I have made one human being at least a little wiser, or a little happier, or at least a little better this day."

Charles Kingsley

The truest help we can render an afflicted man is not to take his burden from him, but to call out his best energy, that he may be able to bear the burden himself.

Phillips Brooks

## Tip of the Day

Do you need a little cheering up? Cheer up somebody else. When you brighten somebody else's day, you brighten up your own day, too.

## Prayer of the Day

Dear Lord, Your love is so wonderful
that I can't really imagine it,
but I can share it . . . and I will . . .
today and every day.
Amen

# Too Much Stuff

Then Jesus said to them, "Be careful and guard against all kinds of greed. Life is not measured by how much one owns."

Luke 12:15 NCV

Are you one of those kids who is lucky enough to have a closet filled up with stuff? If so, it's probably time to share some of it.

When your mom or dad says it's time to clean up your closet and give some things away, don't be sad. Instead of whining, think about all the children who could enjoy the things that you don't use very much. And while you're at it, think about what Jesus might tell you to do if He were here. Jesus would tell you to share generously and cheerfully. And that's exactly what you should do!

If you want to be truly happy,
you won't find it on a never-ending
search for more stuff.

Bill Hybels

Many people today are the slaves of "things"
and as a result do not experience
real Christian joy.

Warren Wiersbe

# Tip of the Day

Too many toys? Give them away! Are you one
of those lucky kids who has more toys than
you can play with? If so, remember that not
everyone is so lucky. Ask your parents to help
you give some of your toys to children who
need them more than you do.

# Prayer of the Day

Dear Lord, sometimes it's easy
to think only of myself, and not of
others. Help me remember that
I should treat other people in the same
way that I would want to be treated
if I were standing in their shoes.
You have given me many blessings,
Lord—let me share them now.
Amen

# Helping People in Need

A person who gives to others will get richer.
Whoever helps others will himself be helped.
Proverbs 11:25 ICB

Lots of people in the world aren't as fortunate as you are. Some of these folks live in faraway places, and that makes it harder to help them. But other people who need your help are living very near you.

Ask your parents to help you find ways to do something nice for folks who need it. And don't forget that everybody needs love, kindness, and respect, so you should always be ready to share those things, too.

Let my heart be broken by the things
that break the heart of God.

Bob Pierce

We hurt people by being too busy,
too busy to notice their needs.

Billy Graham

# Tip of the Day

Where can you share? Look around. Soon,
you'll have a chance to share a helping hand
or a kind word. So keep your eyes open for
friends who need your help, whether at home,
at church, or at school.

## Prayer of the Day

Dear Lord, let me help others in every
way that I can. Jesus served others;
I can too. Today, I will share
my possessions and my prayers.
And, I will share kind words with
my family and my friends.
Amen

# Pray about It!

Do not worry about anything.
But pray and ask God
for everything you need.

Philippians 4:6 ICB

If you are upset, pray about it. If you're having trouble sharing, ask God to help you. If there is a person you don't like, pray for a forgiving heart. If there is something you're worried about, ask God to comfort you.

As you pray more and more, you'll discover that God is always near and that He's always ready to hear from you. So don't worry about things; pray about them. God is waiting . . . and listening!

The man who kneels to God can
stand up to anything.

Louis H. Evans

There is nothing surer on this earth than
the truth that God hears
and answers prayers.

Leanne Payne

## Tip of the Day

Open-eyed prayers: When you are praying,
your eyes don't always have to be closed. Of
course it's good to close your eyes and bow
your head, but you can also offer a quick
prayer to God with your eyes open. That
means that you can pray just about any time.

# Prayer of the Day

Dear Lord, help me remember
the importance of prayer.
You always hear my prayers, God;
let me always pray them!
Amen

# What Jesus Shares with You

For God loved the world in this way:
He gave His only Son, so that everyone
who believes in Him will not perish
but have eternal life.

John 3:16 HCSB

Who's the best friend this world has ever had? Jesus, of course! When you invite Him into your heart, Jesus will be your friend, too . . . your friend forever.

Jesus has offered to share the gifts of everlasting life and everlasting love with the world . . . and with you. If you make mistakes, He'll still be your friend. If you behave badly, He'll still love you. If you feel sorry or sad, He can help you feel better.

Jesus wants you to have a happy, healthy life. He wants you to be generous and kind. He wants you to follow His example. And the rest is up to you. You can do it! And with a friend like Jesus, you will.

I have a Friend in high places.

Anonymous

Christ's love is like a river
that never stops flowing.

Jonathan Edwards

# Tip of the Day

When in doubt, think about Him. When you
have an important decision to make, stop for
a minute and think about how Jesus would
behave if He were in your shoes.

## Prayer of the Day

Dear Lord, thank You for Your Son.
Jesus loves me and He shares so much
with me. Let me share His love
with others so that through me,
they can understand
what it means to follow Him.
Amen

# Bible Verses to Memorize

# God loves the person who gives happily.

2 Corinthians 9:7 ICB

# Honor your father and your mother.

Exodus 20:12 ICB

Trust the Lord with
all your heart. Don't depend on
your own understanding. Remember
the Lord in everything you do.
And he will give you success.

Proverbs 3:5-6 ICB

# Draw near to God, and He will draw near to you.

James 4:8 HCSB

I have come that they may have life, and that they may have it more abundantly.

John 10:10 NKJV

# Thanks be to God
# for his indescribable gift!

2 Corinthians 9:15 NIV

# Unfailing love surrounds those who trust the LORD.

Psalm 32:10 NLT

Show respect for all people.
Love the brothers and sisters
of God's family.

1 Peter 2:17 ICB

# You are the light of the world.

Matthew 5:14 NIV

Above all, love each other deeply, because love covers a multitude of sins.

1 Peter 4:8 NIV

# Do not neglect the spiritual gift that is within you....

1 Timothy 4:14 NASB

So let us try to do
what makes peace and
helps one another.

Romans 14:19 NCV

Jesus said,
"Don't let your hearts be troubled.
Trust in God, and trust in me."

John 14:1 NCV

A joyful heart makes a face cheerful.

Proverbs 15:13 HCSB

...whoever lives and believes
in me will never die.

John 11:26 NIV

# For to me to live is Christ, and to die is gain.

Philippians 1:21 KJV

If I speak with human eloquence
and angelic ecstasy but don't love,
I'm nothing but the creaking
of a rusty gate.

1 Corinthians 13:1 MSG

Love one another deeply,
from the heart.

1 Peter 1:22 NIV

# Love is patient; love is kind.

### 1 Corinthians 13:4 HCSB